J E
Gai
Top
amphibians for kids

$23.93
ocn182621470
10/01/2008

AMERICAN HUMANE

Protecting Children & Animals Since 1877

Top 10 Reptiles and Amphibians for Kids

Ann Graham Gaines

Enslow Elementary

an imprint of

Enslow Publishers, Inc.

 40 Industrial Road
Box 398
Berkeley Heights, NJ 07922
USA

http://www.enslow.com

AMERICAN HUMANE

Protecting Children & Animals Since 1877

Founded in 1877, the American Humane Association is the oldest national organization dedicated to protecting both children and animals. Through a network of child and animal protection agencies and individuals, the American Humane Association develops policies, legislation, curricula, and training programs to protect children and animals from abuse, neglect, and exploitation. To learn how you can support the vision of a nation where no child or animal will ever be a victim of willful abuse or neglect, visit www.americanhumane.org, phone (303) 792-9900, or write to the American Humane Association at 63 Inverness Drive East, Englewood, Colorado, 80112-5117.

Enslow Elementary, an imprint of Enslow Publishers, Inc.

Enslow Elementary® is a registered trademark of Enslow Publishers, Inc.

The top 10 reptiles and amphibians are approved by the American Humane Association and are listed alphabetically.

Library of Congress Cataloging-in-Publication Data

Gaines, Ann.
    Top 10 reptiles and amphibians for kids / Ann Graham Gaines.
        p. cm. — (Top pets for kids with American Humane)
    Includes bibliographical references and index.
    Summary: "Provides facts on the top ten reptiles and amphibians for kids and how to care for them"—Provided by publisher.
    ISBN-13: 978-0-7660-3074-9
    ISBN-10: 0-7660-3074-1
    1. Reptiles as pets—Juvenile literature. 2. Amphibians as pets—Juvenile literature.   I. Title. II. Title: Top ten reptiles and amphibians for kids.
    SF459.R4G35 2008
    639.3'9—dc22
                                        2007047884

Printed in the United States of America

10 9 8 7 6 5 4 3 2 1

To Our Readers:
We have done our best to make sure that all Internet Addresses in this book were active and appropriate when we went to press. However, the author and publisher have no control over and assume no liability for the material available on those Internet sites or on other Web sites they may link to. Any comments or suggestions can be sent by e-mail to comments@enslow.com or to the address on the back cover.

♻ Enslow Publishers, Inc., is committed to printing our books on recycled paper. The paper in every book contains 10% to 30% post-consumer waste (PCW). The cover board on the outside of each book contains 100% PCW. Our goal is to do our part to help young people and the environment too!

Cover Photo: Vic Pigula/Alamy
Interior Photos: Alamy/Design Pics Inc., pp. 2, 28 right; Alamy/Brian Elliott, pp. 3, 25; Alamy/Paul Wood, p. 4; Alamy/Michael Soo, p. 8; Alamy/Arco Images, pp. 10, 36, 40; Alamy/plainpicture GmbH & Co. KG, p. 13; Alamy/Juniors Bildarchiv, pp. 16, 43; Alamy/Chris Mattison, p. 22; Alamy/Ralph Henning, p. 26; Alamy/Kris Mercer, p. 27; Alamy/Brent Ward, p. 30; Alamy/blickwinkel, p. 33; Alamy/Rick & Nora Bowers, p. 38; Alamy/Linda Kennedy, p. 41; Alamy/Olaf Doering, p. 45; Animals Animals–Earth Scenes/Zigmund Leszczynski, p. 11; Getty Images/GK Hart/Vikki Hart, p. 32; iStockphoto.com/Sebastian Duda, p. 1; iStockphoto.com/Heinrich Volschenk, pp. 5, 9, 17, 42; iStockphoto.com/Manuel Angel Diaz Blanco, p. 19; iStockphoto.com/Julie de Leseleuc, p. 23; iStockphoto.com/Eric Isselée, pp. 24, 31, 37, 46; iStockphoto.com/John Pitcher, p. 28 left; iStockphoto.com/Erik Lam, p. 34; iStockphoto.com/Arnaud Weisser, p. 47; iStockphoto.com/Nick Vachris, p. 48; Photo Edit/David Kelly Crow, p. 15; Photo Edit/Kayte M. Deioma, p. 20.

Contents

Reptiles and Amphibians Are Great Pets!

If you are thinking about getting a pet, how about a reptile or amphibian? They make excellent pets! The number-one reason is that reptiles and amphibians are so unique and exotic. In other words, they are very unusual.

Reptiles and amphibians are very interesting animals. Their activity can be

◀ Ball pythons and other reptiles are fascinating creatures to have as pets. So are amphibians, their close cousins.

fascinating to watch. If you choose a reptile or amphibian for a pet, you will be learning all the time!

What Are Reptiles and Amphibians?

Reptiles are cold-blooded animals. This means they get heat to warm their bodies from their environment (from the sun, for example). In contrast, humans and other mammals produce their own body heat. Reptiles include snakes, turtles, and lizards.

Amphibians are also cold-blooded. But unlike reptiles, they have gills for breathing. Salamanders, newts, frogs, and toads are all amphibians.

First, you must get the facts about what it is like to have a pet reptile or amphibian. You can get information from many places. One is a veterinarian (vet). Another is a herpetological (her-puh-tuh-LODGE-uh-cull) society. This is a club whose members study reptiles and amphibians.

Once you have the facts, you can decide whether a reptile or amphibian is truly the right pet for you and your family.

Reptiles and Amphibians Are Great Pets!

There are many things you must talk over with your family. The first thing is that reptiles and amphibians can carry a dangerous disease called salmonella (sal-mo-NELL-a). Owners who are not very careful can get sick from their pets. Because of this, reptiles and amphibians are not the right pets for families with babies, very old people, or people who cannot fight off sickness easily.

Next, can you and your family handle the responsibility? Experts say that kids, even very responsible ones, cannot take good care of a reptile or amphibian all by themselves. From time to time, you will need help from an adult.

You also need to decide if your family can afford to own a pet reptile or amphibian. These pets usually do not cost a lot to buy or feed. However, they may need

A healthy pet tiger salamander can live up to 25 years!

a big cage and other expensive equipment.

Finally, talk about whether your family is prepared to have a pet for many, many years. Some reptiles and amphibians live only a few years. But others can live 25 or 30 years! If your family will no longer be able to care for your pet, it can be very difficult to find it another home. A zoo cannot take it. And it is not fair to your pet to release it into the wild because it will not be able to survive.

Getting a pet reptile or amphibian is definitely a big decision. But if you decide it is the right type of pet for you, and you take excellent care of your pet, it will be very rewarding!

Healthy Reptiles and Amphibians

You have decided to get a reptile or amphibian for a pet. What will it take to keep your pet healthy and happy?

Food and Water

What you may not know is that these animals do not all eat the same type of food. Snakes, for example, are meat-eaters. They need small animals such as mice or insects to eat. One type of lizard called a

▲

The bearded dragon is a reptile that eats both vegetables and meat such as insects. Many other reptiles eat only meat.

uromastyx (yer-o-MAS-tiks), on the other hand, can live on plants alone. Others need both meat and plants to eat.

Reptiles that live in the desert in the wild do not need to drink water every day. But some reptiles and amphibians do need a constant supply of fresh, clean water. Some salamanders need water to swim in as well!

A Home

Pet reptiles and amphibians need a special habitat, or place to live. They can sometimes live in cages. Often it is better for them to live in a terrarium (ter-RARE-ee-um), which is a glass tank like an aquarium.

The best home for a pet reptile or amphibian is a terrarium. It should have places to climb and hide.

▼

These tanks are not filled with water. They are partly filled with dirt or another kind of bedding, and plants. (You can ask to find out exactly what your pet needs.) You will also need to add a place for your pet to hide. Some pets need a place to bask, or soak up light. Some need places to swim, climb, or make a burrow (a hole to hide in).

Some reptiles, especially snakes, can grow to be very large. So it is important to make sure to get a tank or cage that will be big enough for your pet when it is an adult.

Light

Reptiles and amphibians need light—but not just any light. Your pet will need at least one special light, and maybe two! Some need ultraviolet (UV) light. Some also need a heat lamp. Ask your vet what type of lamps to buy and how to use them.

Reptiles and amphibians also need some time in the dark.

Heat

Reptiles and amphibians need both warm and cool spots in their habitat. In some cases, a light can provide the heat they need.

A bearded dragon or other reptile or amphibian's tank needs a light. This will give your pet the light and heat it needs.

▼

But you might have to buy special heating pads or tape.

Health Care

It is hard to tell if a reptile or amphibian is sick. For that reason, your pet will need regular checkups at the vet.

Keeping Yourself Healthy

As an owner of a pet reptile or amphibian, you will need to take steps in order not to get salmonella. You must wash your hands very well with warm water and soap every single time you touch your pet, its food bowl, or its food. You also need to warn your family about this, and watch smaller brothers and sisters carefully. Help them to wash their hands well when they have touched your pet or anything it touches.

It is important to wash your hands very well with warm water and soap after handling any reptile or amphibian.

Also, when feeding your pet, be sure to use tweezers or tongs to give it the food. This way, your pet will not accidentally bite your hand.

Choosing the Pet for You

Now comes the fun part—choosing just the right pet. There are some things to think about while you decide what species, or type, of reptile or amphibian you want.

Is it against the law to own any reptile or amphibian where you live? The laws of your town may say that it is against the law

◀ A bearded dragon is just one of the many kinds of reptiles that make good pets.

to keep a constrictor (a snake that squeezes). In some places, there are laws that say you cannot keep other reptiles or amphibians. To find out about your local laws, have an adult help you contact your city, town, or county animal control office.

Do you want a pet that you will be able to watch a lot? If so, you should get one that is mostly active during the day instead of at night. If you want an animal that will be fun to watch, think about getting a climber, such as a chameleon.

Do you want a pet that you can handle? Some snakes are easy to pick up and carry around. On the other hand, most lizards and salamanders are not. There are a few reptiles and amphibians that cannot be touched at all. For example, oil and salts from our skin are dangerous to salamanders.

▲

A chameleon is very interesting to watch because it will climb around in its tank. It uses its feet and tail to hang on.

What are you willing to do to feed a pet? If you do not like the idea of feeding small animals to your pet, a ball python (snake) will not be the pet for you. For some reptiles and amphibians, you need to raise a supply of insects or worms for them to eat.

Look carefully at the reptile or amphibian you choose. Some pet shops may even help you handle a snake before buying it.

How much money can you spend? Can you afford special lighting, heating, or food? If not, you will have to cross some types of reptiles or amphibians off your list.

Once you have decided what species to get, it is time to find your new pet.

Never try to capture any animal from the wild. Good places to get pet reptiles and amphibians are herpetological societies, rescue groups, specialized pet stores, or breeders. Ask to make sure you are not getting an animal that was captured in the wild. The only reptiles and amphibians that make good pets are those that were born in captivity. In other words, they were born to be pets.

Look carefully at the animal you choose. Make sure it is in good health. Signs of good health are a strong body, skin that is not dull, and clean and clear eyes and nose. Choose an animal that seems lively and alert.

Once you find your pet, you can buy the equipment you will need and create its habitat. Only then are you ready to go get your pet and bring it home!

Ball pythons curl into a tight ball and hide their head when stressed.

Appearance

- Long, strong body with a narrow head
- In the wild, light green or brown in color with yellow belly (breeders have created many new patterns in pet ball pythons)
- Length: females are 3 to 5 feet. Males are 2 to 3 feet.

Diet

Two or three dead mice or rats per week. These can be bought frozen at pet stores, then thawed at home for your snake to eat.

Chapter 1

Ball Python

The ball python is a snake that lives in the grasslands and near rain forests in Africa. It is a constrictor. That means it squeezes its prey to death and then eats it.

Special Needs

A ball python needs a very large tank with a dark place to hide. It also needs clean water in its cage at all times for drinking and soaking. You can handle a ball python, but only after you have washed your hands. Use both hands to support the body but do not hold the snake tightly!

General Behavior

Ball pythons:

1. are curious and gentle snakes.
2. curl into a tight ball and hide their head when stressed.
3. will slither up a tree branch if you put one in their cage.
4. do not move much in colder weather, and may not eat for months at a time!
5. yawn a lot after feeding, to realign their jaws!
6. can live 20 to 30 years.

◀ Ball pythons need water for drinking and soaking. Soaking in water helps the snake shed its old skin.

23

Bearded dragons will often let themselves be picked up.

Appearance

- Wide, flat body covered in spikes
- Triangle-shaped head
- Brown, red, or orange in color
- Length: up to 20 inches

Diet

Young bearded dragons need 20 or 30 crickets three times a day. Adults should also be fed collard greens, kale, or romaine lettuce (ask someone at your supermarket if you do not know what these are or if they are available).

Chapter 2

Bearded Dragon

In the wild, the reptile known as the bearded dragon lives in Australia. It lives in grasslands, the desert, or along the ocean shore. Part of the reason the bearded dragon can live in so many different kinds of places is because it is not a "picky" eater.

Special Needs

Bearded dragons need large tanks. They also like to bask on rocks. Large, natural rocks found outside are best for this.

General Behavior

Bearded dragons:

1. both bask and hide.
2. puff out spikes around their neck when they sense danger.
3. will often let themselves be picked up.
4. are most active when it is warm.
5. can live up to 12 years.

◄ Just one bearded dragon should be kept in a tank. That way, there will be no competition for food.

Chameleons are known for their ability to change color.

Diet

Six or seven live crickets or gut-loaded mealworms every day. (Gut-loaded mealworms are mealworms that you have just fed.) You will need to raise these insects yourself. You can first buy them from a pet store.

Chapter 3

Chameleon

Chameleons are tree-climbing lizards from Africa. They are known for their ability to change color. Scientists believe they turn darker when it is colder, or when they are sick or in danger.

General Behavior

Chameleons:
1. bask.
2. climb on branches.
3. have an interesting walk—they move very slowly and sway from side to side.
4. shoot their tongues out incredibly fast to catch insects.
5. can live 5 to 8 years.

Special Needs

Chameleons need special lighting and just a little water. They are very delicate animals that should not be handled every day.

◀ To have a healthy and active chameleon, its habitat and diet should be controlled very carefully.

Collared lizards run on their hind legs.

Appearance

- Wide head
- Body that narrows to a long, thin tail
- Green in color with scales that are green, tan, or brown
- Two black bands behind the head
- Length: 10 to 12 inches

28

Collared Lizard

The collared lizard is a reptile that lives in the wild in the southwestern United States. It usually lives in rocky areas.

Special Needs

Collared lizards need a large habitat with special heat and lighting. They should not be handled much. As a way to protect themselves, their tails will come off if grabbed. This allows the lizard to get away! The tail will grow back, but it is best not to let your pet be injured this way.

General Behavior

Collared lizards:
1. like to hide.
2. will bask in hot light, then look for shade.
3. run on their hind legs.
4. have lived from 5 to 15 years, depending on their care.

Diet

For young collared lizards, 5 to 10 gut-loaded crickets, mealworms, or earthworms every day. (Gut-loaded means that they have just been fed.) For adults, the same number of gut-loaded insects 3 or 4 times a week. You will need to raise these insects yourself. You can first buy them from a pet store.

◀ In their habitat, collared lizards need a good, shady place to hide as well as a place to bask.

Corn snakes flick their tongues to detect smells in the air.

Appearance

- Small head with long, thin body
- Yellow, orange, or red in color, with patterns of many different colors
- One pattern on the back, and a second pattern on the belly that looks like corn kernels
- Length: about 4 feet

Diet

Two or three dead mice per week. These can be bought frozen at a pet store, then thawed at home for your snake to eat. Smaller corn snakes need smaller-size mice.

Chapter 5

Corn Snake

Corn snakes are found in the wild in many parts of the United States. They live in woods, on rocky hillsides, and often on farms. In the wild, they eat insects, frogs, fish, small mammals, birds, and eggs.

Special Needs

A corn snake will grow over time. Therefore, it is very important to make sure its terrarium is not too small. It will try to escape, so the tank needs a lid that fits tight! Corn snakes also need very clean water and a box to hide in.

General Behavior

Corn snakes:

1. squeeze and suffocate their prey.
2. are gentle in nature and easily handled.
3. like to hide.
4. flick their tongues to detect smells in the air.
5. will try to escape over and over again by pushing up the lid of their terrarium.
6. usually live about 10 years, but some have lived more than 20 years.

◄ In the wild, corn snakes sometimes climb trees. Their ability to climb means they can escape from their terrariums.

Fire-bellied toads spend a lot of their life in the water.

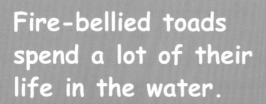

Appearance

- Sturdy body with a round back and large head
- Dark-colored back, sometimes spotted, with brightly colored belly in red or yellow, also with spots
- Big eyes
- Length: 2 to 3 inches

Chapter 6

Fire-Bellied Toad

Fire-bellied toads are amphibians that live in Europe and southern Asia along rivers. There are several different species called fire-bellied toads.

Diet

A few live crickets or gut-loaded mealworms every day. (Gut-loaded mealworms are ones that you have just fed.) You will need to raise these insects yourself. You can first buy them from a pet store. You can also buy guppies to feed your toad every once in awhile.

◀ In the wild, a fire-bellied toad's brightly-colored belly warns predators to stay away.

General Behavior

Fire-bellied toads:

1. spend a lot of their life in the water.
2. show their bellies when they sense danger.
3. catch insects in their mouth (not with their tongue).
4. can live 20 years.

Special Needs

Fire-bellied toads need both wet and dry places in their habitat. Since they have such a long lifespan, be sure to have a plan for the future.

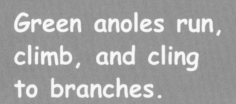

Green anoles run, climb, and cling to branches.

Appearance

- Long, slim body with pointed head, short legs, very delicate toes, and long tail
- Green in color but sometimes change to yellow, brown, or gray. Scientists are not sure why.
- White throat that turns pink when puffed out
- Length: about 6 inches

Chapter 7

Green Anole

The green anole is a small lizard (a reptile) native to the United States. In the wild, it is often seen around houses, on bushes, and low trees. It suns itself on rocks and walls, eats insects such as crickets, and laps water off leaves.

Diet

Two or three live crickets or gut-loaded mealworms every other day. (Gut-loaded mealworms are mealworms that you have just fed.) You will need to raise these insects yourself. You can first buy them from a pet store.

General Behavior

Green anoles:
1. run, climb, and cling to branches.
2. make no sound.
3. drop their tails if they are grabbed.
4. puff out their throats when bothered.
5. can live up to 7 years.

Special Needs

Green anoles need a habitat with special heating. Some may not drink from a bowl. Their owner must spray water on the plants in their tank several times a day to provide a water supply. Green anoles should be handled very little, or not at all.

◀ When it senses danger, a green anole puffs out its throat.

Leopard geckos are active mostly at night.

Appearance

- Long, thin body with pointed head
- Adults are yellow in color, with brown spots
- Babies are striped
- Length: 8 to 9 inches

Diet

For young leopard geckos, several live crickets and gut-loaded mealworms every day. (Gut-loaded mealworms are mealworms that you have just fed.) For adults, several of these insects every other day. You will need to raise the insects yourself. You can first buy them from a pet store.

Chapter 8

Leopard Gecko

The leopard gecko is a lizard native to Afghanistan, Pakistan, Iran, and India. In the wild, they live in dry places such as deserts, or in places where there is just a little grass. In the wild, they eat insects, scorpions—and other lizards!

General Behavior

Leopard geckos:
1. are active mostly at night.
2. live and dig in sand.
3. hide in cool spots.
4. like to live in groups.
5. can live 20 years or more.

Special Needs

Leopard geckos can be hurt if they are not handled properly. It is best to not handle your leopard gecko. Remember the leopard gecko's long lifespan, and have a plan for the future.

◀ If you decide to keep more than one leopard gecko in a tank, make sure you have a special hiding place for each one.

Tiger salamanders can live up to 25 years.

Appearance

- Long, thin body with thick legs and long tail
- Bulging eyes
- Black in color, with yellow spots or bands on the back
- Length: usually 6 to 8 inches, but can grow to 18 inches!

Diet

A few live crickets or gut-loaded mealworms every two or three days. (Gut-loaded mealworms are mealworms that you have just fed.) You will need to raise these insects yourself. You can first buy them from a pet store.

Chapter 9

Tiger Salamander

Tiger salamanders are one of the many different kinds of salamanders. They are all amphibians and can be found just about everywhere in the world. All wild tiger salamanders should be left in the wild.

The best place to get a tiger salamander is from a breeder. If you cannot find one, you should ask at your pet store to make sure that the tiger salamander you want to buy was not captured in the wild.

General Behavior

Tiger salamanders:
1. like to hide.
2. will come to the side of their tank when they see you coming, looking for food!
3. can live up to 25 years.

Special Needs

Salamanders can *never* be handled by humans, not even for a moment. Our skin has oils and salts on it that are dangerous to them. When you first bring your salamander home, put the box it comes in into its habitat and release it without touching it.

◀ Tiger salamanders live in the water when they are first hatched as babies. As adults, they live on land.

Uromastyx are sometimes very shy. Some spend a lot of time hiding.

Appearance

- Narrow head, thick body, and very strong tail
- Yellow, green, or orange in color
- Color changes, according to temperature (lighter in color when it is cool)
- Length: can grow to between 14 and 36 inches

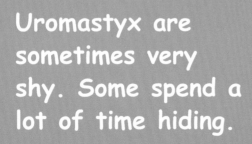

Diet

Dark green salad greens such as chicory, escarole, and kale (ask someone at your supermarket if you do not know what these are or if they are available).

Chapter 10

Uromastyx

Spiny lizards known as uromastyx (yer-o-MAS-tiks) come from the deserts of India, Asia, and Africa. There, they spend their days basking in the sun. They go back to a burrow at night, or when they sense danger.

Special Needs

Uromastyx are healthiest when they are in a very hot and dry environment. Some experts say that in the southwestern United States, they should live in outdoor cages during the summer. However, they will also need cool spots to escape to.

General Behavior

Uromastyx:

1. are sometimes very shy. Some spend a lot of time hiding.
2. may allow themselves to be handled.
3. have lived up to 35 years in captivity. But scientists do not know for sure what a uromastyx's usual lifespan is.

Uromastyx are used to a hot, dry environment. But they also need shady places to hide.

Getting to Know Your New Pet

Before you bring your new pet home, you need to buy and set up its habitat. Make sure to have some food on hand.

After you have made the trip to the pet store or the breeder, bring your pet into the house and place it in its cage or tank. Then what? As hard as it may be, the best thing to do then is to leave the animal alone. Give it time to explore its new home. Of course you will want to look at your pet

When you first bring your pet home, let it get used to its new habitat. Sit back and just watch for awhile.

from time to time. But do not plan on picking it up at least for a few days (if you have chosen a pet that can be handled).

So what will you do instead? Watch your pet from a little ways away. Stay quiet! If you have small brothers and sisters, invite them to watch your pet with you quietly.

From day one, it is important to have a schedule. Every single day, you will need to check on your pet. Depending on what type of animal you have chosen, you may also need to check its water and turn its lights on and off. Since not all reptiles and amphibians need to be fed every day, you will need to make up a special feeding schedule. Once a week you will need to clean your pet's cage or tank. Ask your vet or someone at the place your pet came from what you will need to do to keep your pet's habitat clean.

Within a day or two, take your pet to the vet. Before you go, write down questions you want to ask her or him. This is also a good time to start keeping a pet journal. Write down things you see your pet doing. If your pet suddenly becomes less active you will be able to tell your vet what has been going on. You might also want to write about your pet's habitat. For example, use a thermometer to record the temperature of the basking area.

It can be hard for you to tell if your pet is ill. That is why it is important to bring it to the vet for checkups.

Another reason to keep a journal is because it can help you stay interested in your pet. Remember, a reptile or amphibian may be with you for a very long time. While this means that you have a big responsibility, it also means that you have a great new activity. Become involved in your pet's life. You will become a reptile or amphibian expert!

Glossary

breeder—A person who raises a certain type of animal in order to sell it.

burrow—A hole or tunnel an animal hides in.

captivity—The state of being captured, not roaming freely in the wild.

gills—Parts of an animal's body that allow it to breathe under water.

habitat—An animal's home.

native—Coming from a certain place.

predators—Animals that hunt other animals for food.

prey—An animal that is hunted by another animal for food.

species—A specific type of animal. Animals of the same species can produce young together.

terrarium—A box made of glass that can be a habitat for animals.

veterinarian (vet)—A doctor who takes care of animals.

Further Reading

Bartlett, R.D. *The 25 Best Reptile and Amphibian Pets.* Hauppauge, N.Y.: Barron's, 2005.

Case, Russ. *Lizards.* Irvine, Cal.: BowTie Press, 2006.

Grenard, Steve. *Your Happy Healthy Pet: Bearded Dragon.* Hoboken, N.J.: Howell Book House, 2007.

Grenard, Steve. *Your Happy Healthy Pet: Frogs and Toads.* Hoboken, N.J.: Howell Book House, 2007.

Whiting, Jim. *How to Convince Your Parents You Can Care for a Pet Chameleon.* Hockessin, Del.: Mitchell Lane, 2007.

Whiting, Jim. *How to Convince Your Parents You Can Care for a Pet Snake.* Hockessin, Del.: Mitchell Lane, 2007.

Internet Addresses

American Humane Association
http://www.americanhumane.org

Melissa Kaplan's Herp Care Collection For Kids (of all ages...)
http://www.anapsid.org/mainkids.html

Index